Procrastination

25 Anti-Procrastination Habits on How to Stop being Lazy and Get Things Done

© Copyright 2017 by George Whittaker - All rights reserved.

The following eBook is reproduced below with the goal of providing information that is as accurate and as reliable as possible. Regardless, purchasing this eBook can be seen as consent to the fact that both the publisher and the author of this book are in no way experts on the topics discussed within, and that any recommendations or suggestions made herein are for entertainment purposes only. Professionals should be consulted as needed before undertaking any of the action endorsed herein.

This declaration is deemed fair and valid by both the American Bar Association and the Committee of Publishers Association and is legally binding throughout the United States.

Furthermore, the transmission, duplication or reproduction of any of the following work, including precise information, will be considered an illegal act, irrespective whether it is done electronically or in print. The legality extends to creating a secondary or tertiary copy of the work or a recorded copy and is only allowed with express written consent of the Publisher. All additional rights are reserved.

The information in the following pages is broadly considered to be a truthful and accurate account of facts, and as such any inattention, use or misuse of the information in question by the reader will render any resulting actions solely under their purview. There are no scenarios in which the publisher or the original author of this work can be in any fashion deemed liable for any hardship or damages that may befall them after undertaking information described herein.

Additionally, the information found on the following pages is intended for informational purposes only and should thus be considered, universal. As befitting its nature, the information presented is without assurance regarding its continued validity or interim quality. Trademarks that mentioned are done without written consent and can in no way be considered an endorsement from the trademark holder.

Table of Contents

Introduction 1

Chapter 1: How to Know you have a Procrastination Problem 7

Chapter 2: Why do you Procrastinate and How can you Fix it? 19

Chapter 3: Change your Life for the Better 29

Chapter 4: It's never "Someday" 38

Chapter 5: More Tips to Beat Procrastination 48

Chapter 6: Follow these Steps and Stop Procrastinating Today 54

Chapter 7: Become your Best Self and Achieve your Dreams ... 62

Conclusion 70

Introduction

Congratulations on downloading your personal copy of *Procrastination: 25 Anti-Procrastination Habits on How to Stop being Lazy and Get Things Done.* Thank you for doing so.

Everyone is guilty of being a procrastinator at least once or twice in life, so we are all familiar with it. No one is immune to this phenomenon. Some people are quick or fortunate enough to recognize it when it appears and immediately counteract it. For the rest of us, however, procrastination can steal our dreams away and have a highly negative impact on our quality of life. Reasons for procrastinating vary from individual to individual and isn't always completely obvious to recognize. At times, the act of procrastinating is a subtle fear that we ignore, and at others, it's just a matter of not feeling like doing the right thing.

How can Procrastination Ruin your Life?

This isn't just a dramatic expression; procrastination really can ruin your life. Whichever reasons you have for procrastinating, if you know that you have this habit, you need to face it. This can lead to more damage than it seems, and learning new habits is not as hard as you think. Let's look at some reasons why procrastination can be bad for you in multiple ways.

- **You can't get Time Back:** People often think that money is the most precious thing in the world, but the fact is that time is the most precious commodity any of us are given in life. Procrastination causes you to lose it. How much of your time have you given to procrastinating? Maybe it's hard to tell, but you should be able to have a rough idea by thinking it over. One of the most insidious factors of procrastination is the fact that you can stop and realize that five or 10 years just passed and you haven't changed a bit.

  This feeling is horrible because you are bemoaning something that you can never change. None of us have a time machine (yet) and you will have no choice but to live with the horrible feeling that you wasted precious days and hours of your life. Nothing is worse than that feeling of frustration where the only one to blame is yourself for not taking the first step to action. Don't allow yourself to be subjected to this when it's easy to make the changes needed to live your life in the way you truly want to.

- **You won't Achieve your Goals:** Procrastination appears to be at its strongest when you start to think of your personal goals of changing or achieving something. Maybe you really want to change, but somehow you feel frozen in place, unable to make that first small adjustment. This can get confusing. You may wonder, time and time again why you can't seem to move yourself to act on something you desire more than anything. You can find the answer to this question, but first, you have to explore the resistance you are feeling to change.

People make goals in the first place because they want to better themselves in one way or another. If you miss out on this desire, due to procrastinating too much, you'll destroy your chances at becoming a better person with a better life. You need to start being real and honest with yourself. Get to the root cause of your procrastination or your goals will never be within reach.

- **You're missing One-Time Opportunities:** Procrastinators miss out on valuable opportunities because they don't take advantage when they can. They then spend the rest of the day, month, year, or even their whole lives regretting what they didn't do. What you may not recognize is that the chance you passed up might have been a huge turning point for you, but you gave it up. The majority of big opportunities like this come around only one time; that's what makes them so valuable, and you aren't ever guaranteed another chance to try again. Opportunities should be taken advantage of, not ignored or put off until "later."

- **Your Career could Suffer:** Your methods of working have a direct effect on the results you see from it, along with your quality of performance and the amount you achieve. Perhaps your struggles with procrastination keep you from achieving deadlines or meeting your monthly numbers at work. It seems like a small matter now, or just a few isolated incidents, perhaps, but what will this lead to down the road?

You may be losing out on a chance to be promoted, or you might even get fired when someone without this problem comes along. You can only avoid this harsh truth for so long. The habit of procrastination will definitely ruin your job at some point, and it would all be for nothing.

We will go into more detail about the dangers of procrastination later in this book, but the most important point to make is that you *can* change this habit and tendency in yourself once you decide to do so. Keep in mind that since procrastination is just a habit you've acquired, it's difficult to change, but it affects everything about your life.

What will you Gain from this Book?

Fortunately for you, you have the desire to change, which is the first step to getting better at this. The following chapters will discuss some of the many ways you can take back control over your own life, do the things you want to do, and create the life you wish to have. The book will start with some introductory information on the harmfulness of procrastination and what you stand to gain from changing this habit tin yourself.

Then we will move onto the 25 valuable tips you can put into action to change this, starting today. We are shaped by our choices, every single day, so don't miss out on the chance to become the best version of yourself you can be by stopping this habit of procrastination. Quitting procrastination will:

- **Help you get Out of your Rut:** Those who procrastinate are stuck in a rut. There are no exceptions to this. This means that there is some situation in your life that requires action, and no matter how much you plan to take action or talk about it, it won't happen until you stop procrastinating. When you learn how to quit procrastination, you will exit the stagnant state you're in and grow immensely.

- **Gain better Time Management Skills:** You might often feel as though there isn't enough time in the day, but that's probably because you're wasting it procrastinating! When you quit this harmful habit, you will have a lot more free time immediately that you can dedicate to whatever you feel like doing. When you procrastinate, you create mental clutter. Stopping procrastination will free you from all of that baggage.

- **Face Fears and become a Risk-Taker:** The more you procrastinate with facing challenges, the larger your fear will become. To the procrastinator, even the simplest of actions seem like insurmountable challenges. Break this habit and start to achieve the tasks you need to do, and a whole new world will open up before your eyes. As you can see, you have nothing to lose by doing this, and everything to gain. Let's look at some other benefits you will receive in the following pages of this valuable book.

What else will you Learn?

You will learn more about the points listed in the section above, along with more techniques to quit procrastination in the following chapters. The final chapter of this book will explore proven methods for beating this, along with more information you can use to better your life and self. Thanks again for downloading *Procrastination: 25 Anti-Procrastination Habits on How to Stop being Lazy and Get Things Done* and I hope you enjoy it!

Chapter 1: How to Know you have a Procrastination Problem

Procrastinators don't trust themselves and eventually may even lose their self-respect. Sadly, anyone who is close to a procrastinator will also learn, over time, that they cannot rely on them to do what they say they will. Since trust and reliability are the foundation of all healthy relationships (both professional and personal), this is not a good thing. While some of you may already be 100 percent certain that you have a procrastination problem, others may be in denial or only have a vague suspicion of the issue. If this is you, you need to learn more to find out whether you truly have a problem with this that needs to be worked on. If you bought this book, chances are, you do.

Habits of Chronic Procrastinators:

Below we are going to list some habits that chronic procrastinators have. If you recognize yourself in these, it's time to start taking action now. Not later today, not tomorrow; now! Let's take a look at some signs:

- **You rise Late in the Mornings:** You keep telling yourself that you're going to do something later, then you suddenly notice that it's already evening. You decide to pull an all-nighter to get what you need to get done accomplished. All of a sudden, it's the following day and you've still accomplished nothing. When you first wake up in the morning, you aren't excited to start the day and instead feel like groaning, falling back asleep, or simply avoiding the day altogether. Does this sound familiar?

- **You don't have a real Schedule:** When you aren't sure when you should sleep or what time to wake up, it's easier to procrastinate throughout the day. Perhaps you don't even have a real schedule to get your work or schoolwork done, and you think that getting up at any time of day is fine. This is fine for some of the time, but if this is regular life for you, it's not a good sign. Prioritizing your time shows that you value it and have goals to achieve.

- **You have a lot of Addictions:** Nail biting, drinking, or eating helps you feel calmer when you are stressed, and you tend to do these habits as a way to avoid what you know you *should* be doing instead. Before you know it, you are addicted to social media, soda, and maybe even cigarettes. Anything that will help you avoid what you know you need to do.

- **You usually Give up when it gets Hard:** You like to have "fresh starts" and appreciate new beginnings, but as soon as you get bored, you're more likely to throw in the towel than you are to stick with the path you decided on.

You think of all you haven't accomplished yet and feel so guilty that you're overwhelmed and decide it's easier to forget about the whole thing.

- **You don't Trust yourself anymore:** You can't ever manage to keep your promises, especially the ones you make yourself. Maybe you still make them and kick yourself each time you don't keep them, or maybe you've accepted defeat and have decided to stop making promises you can't ever keep. If this sounds like you, you definitely have a problem with putting things off until "later" or just avoiding them altogether.

- **You're jealous of Hard-Working People:** You have a bit of envy for people who have organization skills and can kick themselves into gear. Even though you admire them, the belief you have that you can't be that way makes you jealous. It makes you feel as though there is something fundamentally wrong with you compared to these other people. This just leads you to procrastinate even more and feel even worse, strengthening the cycle.

- **Life follows a Predictable Pattern for you:** Procrastination has become a deeply rooted habit within you and you usually know exactly how your day is going to go before it starts. You are aware of what is possible and what isn't and you have found it impossible to beat your own self-sabotaging habits. Almost every circumstance you meet seems familiar.

- **You don't Exercise or Stay Healthy:** If you haven't seen the inside of a gym in a decade, you have a procrastination problem. When you don't have good habits of eating or sleeping, you can only dream of becoming fit. Maybe you're skilled with making new plans for getting fit and healthy, but when the time comes, you don't actually stick with it when it counts.

- **You are Constantly Rushing and Disorganized:** Being early or doing things ahead of time is really boring, so you usually wait until the last minute. Whether it's getting that shopping done that you've been putting off, or just finishing your week's work, being early instead of late on deadlines seems nearly impossible for you and you always kick yourself for this. You also have a problem with disorganization in your room or work office.

- **You get Stressed out Easily:** People who have messy lives get stressed out at the smallest thing. This is because they have long since learned that they are "incapable" of getting things done quickly and efficiently. Little do they know that they are only adding fuel to the fire by procrastinating more in response to this. When you find yourself getting stressed out at the first sign that you might have to stick with a schedule, you're probably a chronic procrastinator. You imagine a life of relaxation and it doesn't seem as though it could be a reality for you.

- **You find Excuses to Wait just a "Little Longer":** When you promised yourself the night before that you would wake up at 6 in the morning and wake up to see that it's 5:57 am, you lie in bed and wait for the alarm to go off instead of getting a head start on your schedule. You might even shut your alarm off to go back to sleep or repeatedly hit snooze, instead of getting up when you promised yourself you would.

How often do you Distract yourself?

When you're a procrastinator, you love playing Packman, solitaire, or even games that you think are boring deep down. This is because you would rather do anything than what you know you should be doing. You're great at giving others good advice, but don't follow it yourself. You find yourself wishing, more than anything, that you could just develop self-discipline. This is probably the biggest sign of all that you have a serious chronic procrastination issue. Be honest with yourself about this.

Looking Deeper into the Habit of Procrastination:

Humans are naturally creatures that avoid pain however possible; it's in our very nature. We try to stay away from what we do not like or find uncomfortable or painful, and instead go after what we think will lead to happiness and pleasure. Many times, this human quality results in the habit of procrastination. But when we give into this and procrastinate by letting ourselves indulge in avoidance, it leads to even more pain in the future. Waiting to visit the doctor, putting off paying your bills, and waiting until the night before your taxes or homework are due to finish them are all examples of this. We know that it can lead to serious consequences, so why don't we change?

- **How the Cycle is Created:** Procrastination means avoiding your personal obligations and when you get away with it over and over again, it reinforces your lack of self-discipline and creates a cycle of habit. The way you're raised also matters a lot with your procrastination habits. People who have parents who do too much for their kids, not letting them figure things out on their own, might end up having a procrastination habit later on in life. This is because the child never learns how to be independent and in control of themselves.

- **Waiting too Long:** As stated earlier, procrastination is not just a little harmless habit and can, in fact, ruin lives.

Specific types of procrastination can even have detrimental effects on one's physical health or psychology. For example, people who need psychiatric or medical care and keep putting off visiting a doctor for fear of bad news. This only exacerbates the situation and allows the condition to worsen, all because the patient procrastinated when the issue could have been fixed sooner.

Procrastination often becomes serious enough to become permanent and is even, in some cases, a symptom of OCD. Individuals can get so obsessed with minute details of tasks that they get overwhelmed before they have even begun. This can be combatted by focusing singularly on the actions you need to fulfill throughout the day. We will discuss this in more detail later.

Where does this Tendency Come from?

Styles of motivation in humans develop when we are young, and many link the style they have to their memories of fulfilling tasks like chores or school work. The early responses you had to the related emotions that motivated you, such as motivation to clean your room or complete school work, will still influence you as an adult. You might think that you did these tasks because you had to, only thinking about the thoughts related like "I should do my homework." But there was definitely an emotion present that drove you to either do it or not do it.

Is there anything from your past that you think contributed to your current habits? Experiences like these can deepen and solidify into a habit of either doing things right away or procrastinating. What experiences might you have had related to this that have shaped your motivational style? Looking into this can help you get to the root of the issue and beat it. If you aren't sure whether this applies to you, you can take some time to do some free writing about it in your journal, write out a list, or simply take some more time to reflect and meditate on it a bit more.

Procrastination's Effect on Studies:

Procrastination is not just a bad habit like chewing your nails. It's a far bigger deal than that and is a major factor in students having a hard time at school. The subject is so prevalent and such an issue that countless books have been written on it and studies are always being done on the subject. Procrastinating as a student may be hurting you more than you believe it will.

- **Lower Grades and Higher Stress:** In numerous studies conducted on the subject of procrastination over the previous two decades, it's become quite obvious that this is a harmful habit. It isn't only a bad habit. It has a bad impact on your self-esteem, emotional state, and of course, your grades. Research has shown that procrastinating students received lower grades in school and experienced higher instances of illness and general stress. Not only did they turn their work in later or simply wait until the last minute to get it done; the work's quality was lower and their own state of mind suffered, as well.

- **Committing to Lasting Change:** Education is important and often very expensive, so if you're a student who has a procrastination problem, it's time to tackle it now. Lower stress levels and better grades are something that every student wants. Every time you procrastinate on something important, you are giving up a chance to truly learn and instead forcing yourself to have to "cram" (something most students are familiar with). This seems fine on the surface, but this is not an effective way to store information. Staying away from procrastination instead will allow you to truly soak in and absorb the information you're being taught.

The Role of Social Media in Procrastination:

Websites like Facebook and Twitter have a huge impact on levels of procrastination. It's becoming more and more common that office workers who should be focusing on a project due the next day are instead scrolling through their news feed or watching cute cat videos. The reason for this is simple; when people have more access to various sites and the information they hold, it gives them a quick, gratifying boost to do so. This opens the door for all kinds of procrastination and avoidance. How can you get this under control? Let's look at some ideas for that.

- **Turn your Internet Off:** Oftentimes, the internet is only a small portion of what we need to do for work or school, such as research for a project. After that, it only serves to distract us. You might even find that you sit down with the intention to get a few hours of work done and before you know it, the morning is gone and you've typed less than a page. Take control of this tendency in yourself and any time you sit down to work or write a paper, turn off your internet.

- **Block Facebook and Other Distractions:** There are countless apps out there that have been developed to help people with the distraction of social media. Install an app that only allows you to visit distracting sites for a half hour a day, instead of allowing you to scroll them endlessly. You can also install something called the Facebook news feed blocker that allows you to sign in and check messages, but not to see your news feed. It's too easy to get distracted and scroll for hours on Facebook, so take some measures to prevent this.

- **Keep your Phone Away from your Desk:** When you're trying to work or get some studying done, don't keep your smartphone near you since this is just inviting distraction with open arms. Instead, make sure it's turned off, in the other room, or otherwise far away from you. This will help you resist the temptation to check it again and again when you should be working instead. Digital entertainment devices, although sometimes helpful for staying on task, are usually just the enemy of being productive. Realize this and take action accordingly so you can improve your ability to achieve your tasks throughout the day.

- **Reset your Mind with an Internet Fast:** More and more these days, we're seeing information about how important it is to "unplug and recharge." This gives your mind a chance to recover from the relentless distraction of social media and form healthier, lasting habits. Commit to taking a fast from the internet so you can reassess how much you're really using it to procrastinate and distract yourself when you should be getting things done.

Technology is a great tool that allows us many advancements and conveniences, but used wrongly and it only enables procrastination in the worst way possible. First, you must recognize that this happens and then take actions against it.

Following the steps above will help you stop using technology in negative ways and start using it to better yourself.

Chapter 2: Why do you Procrastinate and How can you Fix it?

Distractions are never far away from us in this digital, modern age. There is never any shortage of reasons to put things off, avoid your work, or procrastinate in general. Instead of giving into this or feeling powerless to stop it, commit now to not wasting one more moment excusing your behavior. Are there some to-do tasks you're putting off until later right at this very moment? Keep reading to find out exactly why you need to change this, and how to do so.

More Reasons to Stop Procrastinating:

- **Procrastination means Taking the Easy Road:** You put off tasks when you find something difficult or challenging in some way. Rather than standing up to the task and completing what you need to get done, you instead seek out insignificant, small activities to distract you and tell yourself that you're being productive. No one enjoys the idea that they are sailing down the easy road, so log out of Twitter and go after what you know you have to do.

- **Keep the Future in Mind:** It's easy to make bad decisions when you're only thinking about today. When you think of it in terms of building lifelong habits and constructing your future, however, it's a bit different. It may seem kind of dramatic, but thinking of life in terms of your future and what you're giving up can help you keep the small tasks you're putting off in the correct perspective. At times, tasks like getting a project done or turning in your work on time seem insignificant or like they don't really matter much. However, keeping in mind that every small task creates our future will give us the motivation we need to stop procrastinating.

- **Stop Procrastinating to be Healthier:** Scientists have found, interestingly, that a link exists between procrastination and harmful issues like cardiovascular disease and hypertension. Although the exact reason why is not clear, the researchers conducting the study believe that those who procrastinate tend to punish themselves when they don't finish projects or have control over their own actions. This perpetual state of stress can lead to health issues.

- **Do better Work:** All people, regardless of how good they are at what they do, are aware that doing things at the last minute will never have as quality of results as actually doing something right. Doing something earlier gives you a chance to do multiple drafts, check for errors, and review the final result. No matter how tempted you might be to believe you can afford to procrastinate, just do what you have to do ahead of time so that when you finally turn in your work, you can be proud of it.

- **Have more Time for Leisure and Fun:** Whenever you procrastinate, you're letting yourself gain a reward in the short term instead of respecting and securing your future. When you do this perpetually, you have less time for your friends, family, and loved ones. Your precious minutes and hours are wasted trying to catch up and fix mistakes when you would have had more free time if you had just done things right the first time around. As you can see, procrastination truly lowers your quality of life over time and stops you from fully enjoying it.

- **Be Proud of your Life:** Procrastination is the number one cause of people's stress, according to research. Studies show that high stress levels come from not finishing things that you know you should, or leaving projects undone. This is why people with this horrible habit often complain about being tired all the time. Putting off tasks that you must do creates huge levels of stress in your life leading to issues sleeping or ever fully relaxing. No wonder it makes people feel exhausted!

The more you ignore important tasks, the more you are adding to your subconscious stress levels. This then lowers your immunity levels and leaves you more susceptible to infections and harmful viruses. You won't be able to concentrate as well, leading to more accidents and absent-mindedness. In serious cases, you might even eventually suffer from depression or other mental issues.

Some people procrastinate just in certain areas of life, such as relationships, while they are efficient in other areas. Some procrastinate in multiple areas of life, such as job-related areas and self-improvement. When you procrastinate, you are essentially living out a life that states that your own well-being and productivity doesn't matter and isn't important enough to pay attention to. This can harm your mental health, as mentioned, but it can also have financial consequences.

Telling yourself it's not a Big Deal:

When people procrastinate, they don't often think through the seriousness of putting off important tasks. This is a huge problem! They might put off paying their credit card bill and end up in crippling debt, for example. This doesn't just harm you, but can negatively impact your partner, children, and family members. We are going to look a bit more into this problem and explore it from many angles, then you will receive some actionable tips for changing your habit.

Looking Deeper into the Issue:

Before you will be able to fix this issue in yourself, you have to first understand the reasons behind why it's such a habit for you. Everyone has their own reasons, but some basic and common reasons are feeling overwhelmed, feeling as though there's no point in trying because the situation won't be affected or changed anyway, or being afraid of failure. Maybe you tell yourself that you're too busy to do what you need to do, are too indecisive, feel tired and overworked, or simply don't want to do your work. All of these different reasons can be linked back to the principle of pain and pleasure, which states that people try to avoid pain and gain pleasure.

What we are going to discuss next are methods for overcoming your habit of procrastination and getting rid of the extra baggage and guilt weighing you down related to this topic. Without further ado, it's time to start our 25 tips for getting rid of the habit of procrastination.

Procrastination Prevention Tip Number One: Get Moving.

One quick and surefire way to get out of your procrastinating mindset is to give yourself a new location. Instead of sitting on your computer or watching television for hours, get moving.

This can mean going outside for a jog, taking a bike ride, or even just doing jumping jacks in place inside of your apartment. Motion helps our brains snap out of a stagnant state of mind. This allows your ideas to flow more freely. Research has proven that the human mind is more creative while in motion than while sitting still, so act accordingly.

Procrastination Prevention Tip Number Two: Give yourself Reminders.

Set hourly or daily reminders that you have a goal you need to dedicate time to. You can do this with a digital app or go the old fashioned route about put up post-it notes where you're sure to see them. Some may gain extra motivation from nice quotes that they can see throughout the day, while others might benefit more from the "tough love" approach, such as setting your alarm with a bossy message to get moving right away. You might also benefit from setting up text or email alerts that notify you throughout the day to complete important tasks or get back to work when you start slacking off.

Procrastination Prevention Tip Number Three: Team Up.

Having someone there to cheer you on and share your joys and struggles is irreplaceable in many areas of life, and this also applies to beating your procrastination habit. Having an accountability partner will help you stay on track because when you fail, you are not only disappointing yourself, but you'll have to tell your partner too.

- **Mutual Motivation:** When you are feeling a lack of discipline, they can cheer you on, and when they're having a hard time, you can offer them that same support. This will fuel a positive reactive cycle that will help both of you reach your goals.

- **Appoint a Friend for your Goals:** Alternatively, you can invite over a family member or friend to come over and oversee you until you finish the task you've been putting off, like finishing your taxes or cleaning your desk out. Ask them if they will kindly sit there and ensure that you get it done. They don't even have to help you beyond this. Once you have finally finished the task, treat both yourself and your friend to a movie, meal, or coffee.

Procrastination Prevention Tip Number Four: Go Public.

It's way too easy to shrug off responsibilities or leave important tasks until "tomorrow" when you only have yourself to disappoint. Instead, try going public with your goals to hold yourself accountable. This can be done with your friends, accountability buddy, or just announced publically as a way to keep you on task. Write about it on your blog or post it to your social media.

Procrastination Prevention Tip Number Five: Do Something Creative Each day.

Creativity has amazing effects on your mind and can help you feel more relaxed and focused on your tasks. Trying to do something creative every single day will help you a lot along this path to meeting your goals and improving your self-discipline. It can also help you get to work on what you've been putting off. You can do some drawing, snap some photos, write in your journal, or play an instrument. Here are some other ideas for awakening the creative spark within you.

- **Join a Dance Class:** Creative movement can be one of the best sources of stress relief in the world. If you already know how to dance, start making more time for it in your life. If you don't, look for a local class that you can join and learn. This can be either a couple's activity to do with your partner or something you pursue on your own.

- **Buy some Paints:** Painting is a great creative activity that is good for the brain and relaxation. If you aren't sure where to start, look online for some tutorials or take a painting class. If you have a friend who knows how to paint, you can also ask them to teach you. Many people are afraid that they simply aren't creative, but that isn't true. Everyone has innate creativity, it's just a matter of finding yours.

- **Learn Graphic Design:** If you enjoy computers and want to find a fun activity you can do digitally, look into learning graphic design. These days, it's possible to learn many different skills online.

Anything that wakes up your brain will help with achieving your goals and quitting procrastination. Understanding what has led to your personal habit of procrastination can be your first step to becoming a changed person and stopping it now. Do you know why you procrastinate? Do you avoid creative activities out of fear of failure? Being creative can be a great way to deal with this. Although they are often related, procrastination is not just about laziness. Let's look deeper into that.

Procrastination is not Always Laziness:

Some people see those who procrastinate and automatically label them as lazy people, but that is far from the whole story. In some cases, that might be true, but in another sense, procrastination is a self-defense mechanism. You're afraid the world will hurt and disappoint you, or that you won't be able to reach the goals you dream of, so you don't even try. It's time to stop letting this rule your life. Don't pretend that this is out of your personal control. You have the freedom to make this change any time you want to do so.

Chapter 3: Change your Life for the Better

Procrastination is the ultimate way that we sabotage ourselves. It's a tactic for delaying what we need to do that can cancel your goals and dreams, completely ruining the grand plans you might have had not only for your day but for your life as a whole. This needs to be taken care of and changed right this instance. This shouldn't be allowed to pause your life and let your dreams crumble. What benefits will quitting procrastination offer you?

Here's what is Waiting for you:

- **The Chance to Discover your Potential:** Do you want to know what you're capable of and just how large your dreams can become? Then you need to quit procrastinating, right now. As soon as you do away with this habit once and for all, you have the chance to become your best self. You will find out what hidden abilities you have, the limits you can stretch to, and more. You will amaze not only others will this, but yourself.

- **Influence Others Positively:** You have innate talents and gifts to help others with, just like everyone else on earth does, and when you give in to procrastination, you allow those talents to fall by the wayside. Every single person has something they can share with the world and influence others in a positive way with. When you decide and commit to no longer procrastinating, you allow yourself to stop holding back from giving your all to the world and the people in it, including yourself. Right now, the world is missing out on what you can offer, but don't let this happen anymore. Commit, right now, to no longer procrastinating and letting yourself reach your highest potential.

- **Achieve Greatness:** Acting in a timely way (the opposite of procrastinating) lets you finally achieve the greatness you've always longed for. Whatever goal you've been dreaming up for the last years must be achieved. Go out there and accomplish it! Finally finish your art project or career goals and you'll be able to proudly add them to the list of what you've accomplished in life. If you're uncertain about what your goals should be, you can ask for help from a friend of yours who you know is great at decision making. As soon as you have decided on a goal, figure out what tasks need to happen to achieve it. Then you can get to work.

- **Discover New and Exciting Things**: When you procrastinate, you end up stuck on the same old things time and time again, because it takes you far longer to complete them than it would have if you had not procrastinated. With each goal you achieve, you are free to move on and discover other exciting and new things. Right now, you probably feel overwhelmed or guilty trying to imagine what new projects you can discover. Doing away with procrastination will let you work on whatever it is you want to without feeling heavy guilt about other issues you've been ignoring and avoiding.

Changing this habit in yourself is all about believing that you can accomplish whatever you need to accomplish. When you feel hopeless, you have to believe that you can change what you want to change and turn your life around, starting now. Get rid of the nagging fear of failure you have and accept that your failures and mistakes can be viewed as valuable learning experiences. There's no shame in going slow and taking your time. Just doing a little bit here and there will add up a lot as time goes on.

Fake it till you Make it:

One major consideration that you should take to heart about quitting procrastination is that sometimes, you have to act like you are confident in order to feel confidence. Eventually, you will act confident enough times in situations to prove to yourself that it's possible to do this. Then, the results of your actions will feed into your self-assuredness, fueling a positive cycle of reinforcement.

Procrastination Prevention Tip Number Six: Become an Early Riser.

One of the best parts about rising early is that it's still and quiet in the mornings, which allows you to focus on what's important. You are able to concentrate just on what you need to, instead of being bombarded with stimuli from every direction as you are when you get up at a typical time. This also gives you a chance to spend some time with yourself and find a calm state of mind to take into the day with you. Some may find this a good time to journal, while their mind is quiet.

Procrastination Prevention Tip Number Seven: Go to bed Earlier.

This ties into the point above, but falling asleep earlier will help you a lot with procrastination. Rising early in the morning isn't possible if you didn't go to bed earlier the night before. You have to give your brain time to recharge, and being sleep-deprived and exhausted throughout the day will only feed into procrastinating even more.

- **No Digital Devices before Bed:** Artificial light disrupts our sleep patterns, so two hours before you go to sleep at night, make a rule that you don't watch TV or use your smartphone.

- **Read Fiction before Sleep:** Reading fictional stories is better than scrolling Facebook before you go to sleep. This helps your mind relax and unwind, paving the way for a good night's sleep.

Your quality of sleep matters a lot in terms of your levels of productivity, so if you've been neglecting this area of your life for a while, it's time to change it and get serious about resting right.

Procrastination Prevention Tip Number Eight: Clean and Organize Along the Way.

At times, we notice that there's a huge mess going on in our personal situation, but rather than facing it and taking care of it, we decide it's a better choice to procrastinate. This is because we're trying to avoid the pain that comes along with facing difficult situations. However, this only makes the situation harder and more complicated. Then we end up beating ourselves up for not taking action, and the cycle continues. Instead of looking at the mess as a whole, try looking at it in smaller chunks. Then take about 20 minutes each day to do something to help the situation. This can mean organizing your house, applying for jobs, or fixing your bad eating habits.

Procrastination Prevention Tip Number Nine: Get Rid of your TV.

Wasting hours in front of your television on a regular basis has very detrimental effects on your procrastination levels. You will save money and get more done by getting rid of your television. If this is too extreme for you, just cancel your cable and hide your TV cord from yourself. It's fine to watch movies or shows every once in a while, but this should be done to reward yourself or as a rare treat, not on a consistent basis.

Procrastination Prevention Tip Number Ten: Just get it Done.

There are countless tips out there for beating procrastination, but none are as simple or effective as this one; just get it done! Stop putting it off and making excuses. Recognize when you're making excuses and decide that you will no longer tolerate that. Take the first step and allow yourself to build positive, productive momentum toward getting your goals achieved. Let's look at some fear-based reasons that you might be procrastinating in your life:

- **Fear of Failing:** At times, even a possibility that you may fail can lead you to avoid the situation altogether, or any task related to it. We fear the change that we might experience pain or discomfort, and so we stay away from new situations and try to remain in our comfortable little bubble of familiarity. However, this is harmful and keeps us from growing or learning throughout life. This then leads to subconscious stress and worsens our procrastination habit. Perhaps you've had a bad experience in the past that is still coloring your current experience or perspective.

But that is simply an excuse not to live fully. Accept that you are using this as an excuse to keep yourself safe and that this fear is unfounded. Without new experiences, you are missing out on a huge chunk of life.

- **Fear of being Successful:** This might sound confusing or doubtful at first glance. After all, who would actually fear being successful? Isn't that what everyone wants? But fear of success does happen. We are afraid of being put into positions of responsibility that we aren't ready for when we are successful. We also fear being put into situations that aren't familiar to us where we might be challenged, embarrassed, or look foolish. In order to get past this, it's important to recognize that this fear exists in yourself. Only then can you work on changing it for the better.

Looking at Life Circumstances that may Cause Procrastination:

What are your personal reasons for this issue? To get this problem under control, you have to look deeper into the reasons behind your habit of procrastination.

- **Mental Causes:** Some put things off habitually because they aren't motivated, don't have energy, or simply don't feel any interest in the activities in their life. If this applies to you, maybe you aren't on the correct life path and need to make some changes. Perhaps you suffer from depression or anxiety problems that make you feel as though you aren't capable or worthy of a good life, so you sabotage yourself by procrastinating. Maybe your negative feelings cause you to feel paralyzed and powerless to pursue the life you really want, causing you to procrastinate on a habitual basis.

- **Lifestyle Causes:** You might be studying a subject that you don't actually care about or be working at a job that doesn't fulfill you. Sometimes, procrastination can have deeper roots, such as these, that can be changed with a little bit of introspection. You might have too many distractions in your life that are feeding into this issue, or perhaps you aren't being healthy and this is causing mental tension that leads you to procrastinate. You might be in an unhealthy or bad relationship that causes you stress and leaves you feeling overwhelmed so that you don't have any extra energy to dedicate to important tasks and instead put them off repeatedly.

- **Not enough Knowledge:** Maybe you don't have enough knowledge to complete your responsibilities or tasks, and this is why you put them off. This all comes down to being lazy and not having self-discipline. Being too ashamed to admit that you don't know is not an excuse to put off fulfilling what you need to do. It's your responsibility to find the information you need to do what you need to do.

Chapter 4: It's never "Someday"

Every procrastinator is familiar with the term "someday", but the fact is that this mythical day never arrives. If you want to overcome your chronic procrastination habits, you need to get clear about your goals and what you desire in your life. If you're a procrastinator, you'll appreciate this next part.

A Quick Exercise for Planning Goals:

- **Make a List:** Take a quick 30 minutes to plan out your goals. Write them down in all or some of the following categories; travel, volunteer, spiritual, physical, relationships, career, etc. The average person will have quite a long list of goals they want to achieve.

- **Minimize your List Items:** As soon as you've made your list, cut it down to just a few items. Ask yourself whether you can live without certain things and allow your less important desires to sit on the list so you can revisit them later on. Delegate or delete anything from the list that doesn't help your top goals and forget about them without looking back. This will help you narrow your focus.

- **Tie Tasks you Resist to your Personal Goals:** The next step is to link the tasks that you dislike or constantly put off to these central goals. It will help you to tie these activities to deep values or goals that you hold. If, for instance, having a clean house lets you have a calmer mind, which is something you strive for, start to value the activity of cleaning and staying organized. Realize that by having a clear head (which results from cleaning and organizing), you will reach your goals quicker and feel happier.

Instead of viewing your choices and tasks as isolated instances, it helps to see them in the bigger picture. What do your actions lead to and what will the end result be? When you link the to-do task to the pleasurable feeling of having a clear, calm mind, you have the motivation you need to do what you have to do. This will help you end your habits of procrastination and get things done.

People can Change when they Decide to:

One of the most impressive and extraordinary traits of human beings is their ability to change and adapt to situations when they put the effort into it. This is what this book is all about; motivating and inspiring people to take action on their desires, instead of feeling powerless. Procrastination is a silent killer, stealing happiness and joy from you. If you have hopes to live happily (which most of us do), you need to do away with this horrible habit. Decide right now that you will drop it.

Procrastination is the absolute opposite of happy and efficient productivity. In order to be productive and contribute to the world, we have to pull our own weight and do our best. Just because this problem is common doesn't mean it's ideal. Let's look at some more tips for getting this under control.

Procrastination Prevention Tip Number Eleven: Mark your Calendar.

Setting up time blocks will help you with getting work done on specific tasks. When you know that something important is coming up, like a big presentation or project, mark it on your calendar and decide that you will work on it on those specific days. This will help you by defining precisely what needs to be done and when instead of just having a vague idea that you need to do something in the future. The more specific you are, the easier it will be.

Procrastination Prevention Tip Number Twelve: Utilize Lists.

There's a reason why the concept of the to-do list is so prevalent and widespread; it's because it works! If you don't already, follow a to-do list every day. It's more difficult to achieve goals when you haven't specifically defined tasks that contribute to meeting them. Keep your list with you at all times to make sure that you are following what needs to be done. If you already use lists, look for ways to make them more efficient and effective.

Procrastination Prevention Tip Number Thirteen: Think of the Consequences.

There are always consequences when you don't do what you know you should do. For example, maybe it's time to renew your vehicle registration but you want to procrastinate on this task.

- **Actions and Consequences:** When you think about skipping the DMV and doing it "later", instead stop and picture what will happen if you don't do what you need to do. You will have to pay fines and risk getting a permanent mark on your record for being caught driving without this documentation. Use this thought of the consequences as motivation to do it.

- **Motivated by Negativity:** Of course it's great to be motivated by positivity, but one amazing fact about human evolution is that humans can also gain motivation to achieve their goals by negative feelings or fear. This is a misunderstood, powerful, and primary motivation source that you can tap into. Most procrastinators are not in touch with this fundamental principle and instead tell themselves not to worry about anything negative. This is how they allow themselves to continue slacking.

How does this principle work in practice? People are usually motivated to take action based on their desire to turn negative emotions into positive ones, or just to feel good in general. This is a fact about the way humans function emotionally and mentally. Whether you realize it or not, this has a lot to do with the actions you perform each and every day. So instead of being cut off from negativity or pretending it doesn't exist, try thinking more deeply about consequences and ways you can feel more positive.

Procrastination Prevention Tip Number Fourteen: No Email Allowed.

All effective workers and goal-setters know that they have to limit the time they spend checking email or wasting time. This is one of the worst activities you can partake in when you're trying to be productive. Your to-do list should be the first thing you jump on in the morning so that you are taking advantage of your clear state of mind instead of getting distracted, which will only make work harder later.

Procrastination Prevention Tip Number Fifteen: Get Rid of your Social network.

Pinterest, Twitter, Facebook, Tumblr, all of these are distractions and just make life harder for a person who already struggles with procrastination. You can do as suggested earlier in the book and simply turn off the internet as you work so you can't access these sites, or if you are really dedicated you can delete them altogether.

Different Types of People and Goals:

Although a lot of successful types of people can't help but perform the tasks they must do immediately instead of putting them off, a lot of other types of people will put off important tasks until they have a deadline hanging over their heads. Those who achieve a lot will put effort into everything they do and wouldn't dream of missing a deadline, even if they work right up until the deadline. What is their motivation? As mentioned earlier, negative consequences are often a motivating factor, but that's far from the entire picture.

- **Their Self-Esteem:** For some, fulfilling responsibilities and taking care of important tasks is deeply entwined with their sense of self-esteem. They might be fueled into action by an image they have of themselves.

- **Rewards:** Another motivating factor that people use to stay on task and achieve their goals is rewards, such as promotions at work or positive attention from those around them.

- **Helping Others:** Other still might be motivated to achieve goals and accomplish tasks by the positive impact their work will have on others.

Getting in Touch with what Motivates you:

Humans are emotional creatures, and there is no shame in admitting that a lot of our actions come from a feeling of some kind, whether it's avoiding pain or seeking pleasure. People who have beaten procrastination have figured out this basic principle and used it to their benefit. Non-procrastinating types of people complete their goals based on which emotions active them most. Even procrastinators who get their work done on time (after waiting until the very last minute) gain motivation from different emotions that get activated when there's an imminent deadline approaching. This is arguably not as good of a motivator since it's based on stress and not a deeper value like helping others or improving one's sense of self.

Finding a Balance between Tasks and Enjoying Life:

Emotions that get in the way of non-procrastinators' success can be hidden oftentimes because although they get their work done, they might not be producing the most optimal results. Along with this, people who feel an urgency toward accomplishing tasks might notice that they are so focused on this that they don't engage with other people or relax as much as they wish they did. It's necessary, then, to find a balance here between achieving the tasks you must do and enjoying life. Here are some guidelines to help with that:

- **Plan your Daily Life:** Your day, every single day, should be planned out, which shouldn't take too long. This will usually only require up to 15 minutes of thought to achieve. Whatever is most important or difficult should be done first so that the rest of your day goes smoother and feels easier to you. You will feel much better if you take this approach to your days. Focus on this in order to get the motivation needed to wait to go online until you're done with your work for the day.

- **Weekly Planning Guidelines:** Planning out your week is important too. This should be done with enough time to schedule time for big goals you need to do. At times, procrastination might occur just because you have yet to officially put something in your schedule. This makes it harder to remember how to do it.

- **Give yourself Breaks sometimes:** Everyone needs a break sometimes, so allow yourself to cheat when necessary. If you have low motivation on one day or feel exceptionally overworked or tired, it's okay to rest a bit, as long as you can recognize when you are making excuses or avoiding important tasks. The great part of beating procrastination is that you'll be able to recognize when you've done enough or not because you will trust yourself and your own judgment.

- **Don't go too Far:** You should always do what you need to do, but it's also important not to go too far. It's easy to overdo it when you get in the one of achieving task after task as fast as you can. A lot of us put unnecessary extra pressure on ourselves to achieve more than we must do, like chores or school work. Remember that your peace of mind is important too! Give yourself breaks and make a schedule that allows you plenty of periods of rest and relaxation in between your goals. Figure out what you absolutely need to do and let go of the image of being perfect at everything. This will ensure that you are not only productive, but happy, healthy, and balanced.

- **Look at the Smaller Steps:** Of course people get overwhelmed when they look at everything they need to do as one gigantic group of tasks. Try, instead, to have a more simple focus and break each goal down into tiny chunks. When you only have a vague idea of something big you need to do, it's too easy to put it off or get distracted. This is because it wasn't important enough to define, so why would you think of it as important enough to take action on? Anytime you feel overwhelmed, this is a great way to calm yourself down and still get things done.

Chapter 5: More Tips to Beat Procrastination

Have you noticed that you only feel a sense of urgency when you have a deadline that is coming up very soon (like the next day)? When your inner-voice only gets serious at these times, it's time to start taking this more seriously and looking deeper at your habit of procrastination. Or perhaps you get caught up on dreaming of the future instead of thinking about the present or taking action in your life right now. When you aren't aware of how you can get motivated to do what you need to do, daydreaming can become a distraction or even addictive. Other people seem to make it easily and you often think it will be easy to do what they do, but when you try, you can't seem to get yourself to do the work involved.

Procrastination Prevention Tip Number Sixteen: Keep Time.

Another method for beating procrastination is setting a timer for yourself as you work. You will be more productive if you work 2/3 of the time and have free time for the other third, then repeat throughout the day. This works better than trying to work for very long periods of time and then taking one long break in the middle. Plus, when you know that you only have to work for

1.5 hour long chunks at a time instead of, say, four-hour chunks, it can be a lot easier to stay on task instead of getting distracted.

Procrastination Prevention Tip Number Seventeen: Keep Track.

You can track yourself to beat procrastination. If you aren't sure how much of your time you're spending with distraction, you can track your time and find out. Find out what your biggest weaknesses are so you can set to work changing them. There are plenty of apps on the market for this very purpose.

- **Use your Calendar:** Calendars are almost outdated technology at this point (at least the ones made of paper) but a classic wall hanging calendar can be of great use to helping you be more productive with your daily tasks. Telling yourself you'll do something "later" or "when you get the time" is just another way of saying it's not important to you. For the things that are, mark them down on this physical device where you can see them every day.

- **Get Real with yourself:** If you want to beat this habit of yours, you have to get real with yourself. Pretending that there isn't a problem or that everything is going to magically fall into place without any effort or work from you is just a big waste of time. As you make your schedule and keep track of your time, pave the way for your personal success. Goals often require more time than we think they will, so make sure you give yourself some extra room. If you know that you are more energetic in the afternoons than the mornings, work with that and schedule your new gym time for the afternoon instead of expecting that you will wake up at five in the morning to do it.

Procrastination Prevention Tip Number Eighteen: Try some Automation.

The most productive people out there know that they should take advantage of our digital world and they automate certain tasks. If there's something that you dread doing on your computer, try to automate it. This can be done with auto-email responses, blog updates, and more, and will let you focus on what you're more interested in.

Procrastination Prevention Tip Number Nineteen: Listen to Motivating Music

What music makes you feel excited, energetic, and motivated when you hear it? Make a playlist that you can jam out to whenever you need to buckle down and get something important done. Music can be a great source of inspiration that you should definitely take advantage of. Here are some other sources of inspiration you can make time for to help you with procrastination:

- **Explore Nature:** Nature is revitalizing for the human spirit, especially when you've been extremely focused on a project or work for a while. Make some time for taking walks outside and breathing in the fresh air, enjoying the trees and greenery, and you will feel re-energized when you return to your tasks. This will then let you get more done and have less time to slack off and procrastinate.

- **Get some Entertainment (when it's Deserved):** Try to focus on entertainment that isn't digital, such as an art museum or a card game with friends. This helps your mind unwind, de-stress, and will help you get more work done when you do return to it. Then you won't have to procrastinate as much.

Procrastination Prevention Tip Number Twenty: Name your Fears.

Procrastinators are often frozen into inaction because they feel some vague, undefined fear that holds them back. Be brave and find out what it is you're avoiding out of fear. Once you identify it, it will be easier to find solutions to beat it. Then you can focus your energy on creativity and work instead of avoidance tactics and procrastination. Don't ever settle for the fact that you have a habit of procrastination. This is not just your nature, it's a habit that can be changed with effort.

How can you Make it Easier?

Becoming more productive is all a matter of finding ways to make life easier on yourself. Whenever a goal or task appears to be overwhelming or overbearing, that's when we tend to procrastinate. So in what ways can you make this easier on yourself and break the goal into more manageable chunks? Let's look at some examples:

- **Writing a Book:** Thinking of the act of "writing a book" sounds intimidating. Writing a paragraph a day, on the other hand, doesn't. You can make this bigger goal (writing the book) easier on yourself by only thinking of the small amount of writing you need to do to work toward this overarching goal. If you end up writing more than a paragraph, great! But there's no need to overdo it at first.

- **Getting Healthier:** What sounds easier, replacing soda with water every day, or suddenly becoming a marathon star who eats nothing but vegetables? Be realistic about your goals. If you want to be healthier, start with small changes you can begin implementing easily and without much struggle. Then you can work your way up to where you want to be.

Many people in psychology believe that procrastinators simply aren't as good at sensing time. In other words, they believe that they have more time than they actually have to get things done and thus put things off. But newer research has emerged that shows that it's more about avoiding something that is believed to be stressful or painful.

Chapter 6: Follow these Steps and Stop Procrastinating Today

Procrastination is draining for your mind, body, and soul. It even makes your memory function sub-optimally! Our memories function at their best when they have enough recovery time to get rid of pressure and decompress. In other words, you have to take breaks if you want your memory and mind to work to their fullest capacity. Some procrastinators fool themselves into thinking that by waiting until the last minute, they are saving time, but in actuality, they are wasting and using more time.

Procrastination Prevention Tip Number Twenty One: Banish the Idea of Perfection.

This sounds counter-intuitive, but procrastination and perfectionism often go hand in hand. You're so worried about doing things right that you don't start them at all out of fear of failing. You need to realize that aiming for perfection only holds you back. Commit to doing your best and let that be enough.

Procrastination Prevention Tip Number Twenty Two: Stay Aware.

When you commit to being more mindful, it's harder to procrastinate. Start paying attention to your surroundings, your breath, your emotions, and thoughts. This will help you make the right decisions when it matters the most. Learning how to meditate can be a great help with this. This is a skill you can learn more about online, listen to guided audio meditations on YouTube, or read some books about. You might also be able to join a local group that will teach you how to meditate.

Procrastination Prevention Tip Number Twenty-Three: Become Single-Minded.

Some believe that multi-tasking is the ultimate sign of productivity when in fact, the opposite is true. In order to produce great results, you should learn how to focus in on one thing at a time. Give yourself a time limit for each thing and get it done.

- **Get Fewer Hours at Work:** A lot of people procrastinate because they have taken too much onto their place and don't even realize it. Take a look at your schedule and goals. If it's overloaded with too many tasks, take an honest approach and cut some things off the list, as mentioned in an earlier tip. Identify the projects that are most important and focus just on those.

This will allow you to feel more relaxed and actually focus on what you need to do instead of feeling frenzied and hurried.

- **Learn to Appreciate the Quiet:** A lot of people, especially in the age of smartphones and social media, have forgotten how to be okay with silence. This contributes to stress, being overworked, and of course, procrastination. Teach yourself to love the quiet, if you don't already appreciate it, then carve out some time each day for this. You should have a minimum of 15 minutes each day dedicated to this, but more is even better. This will allow you to calm down, de-stress, and head back to your work with a sharper focus and deeper motivation.

Procrastination Prevention Tip Number Twenty-Four: Practice Self-Forgiveness.

You may think that self-forgiveness and procrastination are unrelated, but in fact, in order to stop procrastinating, you need to forgive yourself. When you beat yourself up for not doing enough, it only stresses you out more and keeps you locked into the negative cycle you're stuck in. Instead, decide that from now on you won't bear yourself any ill will for your past mistakes, and then do the best you can!

Procrastination Prevention Tip Number Twenty Five: Use Tools Minimally.

For a chronic procrastinator, anything can be used as an excuse to put off more important tasks or goals. Although it's useful to read materials and install apps that are meant to help you get past this issue, be mindful of whether they are becoming just another distraction tactic. Don't let useful tools and ideas distract you from your goals, no matter how good they are. Spend more time by yourself or out in nature so your mind can be free from clutter and the feeling of being overwhelmed.

Do you Recognize this in Yourself?

It's unfortunate enough that this habit can lead to poorer work performance for you, resulting in getting yelled at by your boss, or having to spend your free hours in the office. But habitually delaying important tasks can also impact your immune system and general health, as mentioned earlier in the book. It's been linked to digestive problems, the flu and colds, headaches, and more. What's worse is that people who tend to procrastinate deal with medical emergencies in ways that are harmful and damaging. They might avoid exercise or visiting the doctor, leading to poor health.

- **Avoidance:** One harmful method for coping that procrastinators use is avoiding issues altogether, even when they desperately need to take action. Instead of facing the fact that there is a problem, they would rather pretend that there isn't until it blows up in their face.

- **Self-Blame:** Another negative side effect of procrastination is the tendency to beat oneself up and blame oneself. After disappointing yourself and others so many times, you might become very critical and hateful, berating yourself on a regular basis.

These two habits, and the other problems that come from the bad habit of procrastination will only get worse over time if they are not looked at right now. This is why self-forgiveness is an absolute must for anyone hoping to get past this and make a better life for themselves. If you can't seem to find a good place to start, this is where you should.

How Catastrophizing can Make Procrastination Worse:

For people who struggle to keep themselves on task and, instead, procrastinate all the time despite their best intentions and desires, there are some steps you can take to stop catastrophizing.

- **Stop being so Dramatic:** One major reason why people put things off is because they are thinking very dramatically, or catastrophizing. They imagine how boring or tough something is going to be, like working out or studying, and make it out to be unbearable. Then it's easier to avoid it than actually doing it. When it comes down to it, they are often very wrong and the task they've been avoiding ends up being much easier than they feared. So next time you catch yourself dramatizing a dreaded, "horrible" task, instead tell yourself that it's not that big of a deal and that you can handle it.

- **Find out the Why:** Procrastinators are great at focusing on the moment and not so good at looking at the bigger picture of things. Learn to see the deeper benefits to what you're doing and the lasting advantages it will bring to your life. If you can't seem to focus on work, think about why you're there in the first place. If you've been putting off eating better, imagine the energy you'll have when you finally start being smarter about your nutrition habits.

- **Notice your Excuses**: Do you often tell yourself that you have to be in the right mood to get something one, or that you need to wait until you have more time? Perhaps you tell yourself that deadlines make you work better or that something needs to happen before you will actually get to work on your goals. These are all excuses and you need to start being honest about that, or they will never change and you'll just continue acting in the same old ways.

Allot yourself Undisturbed Time:

If you want to get a handle on your habit of procrastinating, your environment should be optimized for ultimate productivity. We already discussed keeping your phone off or in a different room while you work, or switching off your internet and social media accounts, but you can take this a step further. Ask people that you live with not to bother you during certain times of day that you wish to dedicate to your goals. Use the internet only for work-related research and then turn it off once you have enough.

- **Give yourself Rewards:** Reward yourself when you finally accomplish what you were hoping to accomplish. This can be scrolling Facebook or watching a movie on Netflix. Instead of using these enjoyable leisure activities to avoid your important work or tasks, use them as an incentive to get your work done quicker and more efficiently.

- **Don't Beat yourself up:** We already talked a bit about the importance of forgiving yourself when you have a hard time. Studies show that you can be more efficient and get to work sooner when you forgive yourself for the procrastination you've been guilty of in the past. Telling yourself that you should have begun earlier actually has a counterproductive effect and causes you to put off important tasks for even longer.

- **Mistakes let you Learn:** Acknowledge that your mistakes help you learn more about yourself. We talked a bit about the dangers of perfectionism earlier in the book. Accept that your goals are not either perfect or a complete failure. It's better to get something done than to do something perfectly. Again, some day does not exist, only today!

If you notice that you spend too much time on Facebook, searching for people you haven't seen in years or looking at every notification that pops up, it's time to get real about your procrastination problems. You procrastinate out of fear that you can't achieve something and this just makes you feel even more helpless. Someone who is not productive doesn't know when they should relax and when they should buckle down. Their sense of urgency is very skewed and they are often either completely overwhelmed or fed up. This can all change for you, starting now. Read on to find out more about becoming your best self and achieving your dreams.

Chapter 7: Become your Best Self and Achieve your Dreams

When you procrastinate too much, your self-esteem eventually suffers severely, leading to a vicious cycle of a lack of self-trust and a self-fulfilling prophecy. At times, procrastination comes as a result of already having a poor image of ourselves. Not only does continuing down the path of procrastination reinforce this low self-image; it contributes to it and makes it even worse. You may constantly ruminate on what is the matter with you, wondering why you seem to fail consistency. Not having a healthy self-image can make you suffer in countless different ways.

What Happens with Low Self-Esteem?

When you have a poor image of yourself, you will subconsciously keep yourself from taking chances that could lead you to disappointment. Essentially, this is constant self-sabotage. Then you procrastinate and the results of that lower your confidence levels even more. This will only get worse as time goes on if it isn't addressed and fixed. If all of this sounds familiar to you, you can work on feeling better about yourself and gaining more confidence, and this will also help you stop procrastinating. Let's look at some of the other downsides to procrastination and self-sabotage.

- **Poor Decision Making:** Procrastination leads you to make decisions based on the faulty belief that there is something wrong with you, or that you can't do what you need to do. When you operate from this attitude or default mindset, the results are often going to turn out negative. Every time you put something off or wait until "later", you are making choices based upon a self-belief that is only there because you procrastinate in the first place. Can you see how this cycle can be harmful? When you start to do things right when you know you should instead of later, or worse, never, this pressure disappears. You are finally free to breathe calmly.

- **A Bad Reputation:** When you tell yourself and others that you will fulfill a responsibility or task, and then you don't live up to your promises, your reputation will suffer and no one will respect your word anymore. This is something that no one should want. Apart from causing damage to your personal reputation, you are also hurting your confidence and esteem, along with the way others view you. You might even notice that procrastination seems to get easier and easier since you expect to fail and disappoint others.

Perhaps people have even stopped depending on you altogether or expecting much from you. This means you're holding yourself back from opportunities that might be offered if you and your word were more reliable.

People likely don't want to ask you favors or to take on responsibility because they can't rely on you to do what you say you will. Although this is disappointing and depressing to think about, the good news is that you can change it.

- **Increased Anxiety Levels:** When you are a procrastinator, you are increasing anxiety levels both in yourself and other people. Stress on a consistent and regular basis is bad for you and can cause lasting damage if you don't get it under control. Not to mention that when you are anxious and stressed out, you tend to do a poorer job performing tasks than you would if you were in a calm or rational state of mind. Thus this kind of stress is detrimental all around. When someone is stressed like this on a regular basis, the people around them also suffer because that type of attitude is never fun to deal with consistently. Think about your loved ones and commit to getting this under control before it's too late.

What Else can you do to Help this?

As you work on these steps and tips given to you, you should also follow these guidelines to make sure that you change this habit for good and not only temporarily.

- **Acknowledge your Faults:** You first need to accept and acknowledge that you have a weakness that needs work. Identify the blame you might be assigning to other things, such as your parents or circumstances, and instead become responsible for your choices. This is different than feeling guilty about them. Rather, it's just taking a realistic view so that you can change. You can't change this problem if you don't acknowledge it.

- **Get Specific about how you Procrastinate:** It's easy to notice that you procrastinate, but it can be harder to recognize all of the specific ways that you do this. Get out some paper and make a list of all of the specific ways you procrastinate in day to day life. Then you can find the specific reasons you have for doing so and change them with the tips in this book.

- **Get Specific about the Consequences:** We have gone over plenty of general consequences of procrastination in this book, but you need to figure out how it's negatively impacting you on a personal basis so you can realize that actual impact. Look at the chances you're missing out on, what you've said no to, and decide whether you're really ready to make this step. A vague desire isn't enough to cause lasting change; you must really and truly want it.

- **Refuse to Accept Subpar Efforts:** Tell yourself each and every day that you refuse to procrastinate. Remember the consequences of doing so and realize that when you have things to do, you are going to do them. Make a list if you need to in order to find out what you should do first. Making a plan is essential to your success with this. When you are not prepared, you are destined to fail. Prepare your environment and your mindset by having a list ready.

- **Notice Fear and Look past it:** Changing your life can be scary or make you afraid, but this isn't a reason to avoid changing and growing. Instead, learn to start recognizing when you feel anxious about something and doing what you need to do anyway. This will eventually lead you to feel excited and enthusiastic about your new life and habits.

- **Find Inspiration:** Do you have someone you look up to? This can serve as great motivation to stop procrastinating. Anytime you have the temptation to put something off, remind yourself of how your hero or inspiring figure would act. Try to stay far away from people that have negative beliefs that can impact you in bad ways and instead associate with confident and positive people who will lift you up.

- **Practice Thinking Positively:** Positivity goes a long way. When you have a positive attitude about your ability to change, this is the first step toward actually doing it. Focus on the impact your efforts are going to have. When you focus instead on negativity, this only draws more of it to you and holds you back. Believing that you are capable is the first step in the success you will experience in your life. Take controlling your own mind seriously.

- **Find a Greater Purpose:** It can be hard to stay motivated when you don't know why you're doing it. Having a greater purpose can help you gain the focus and discipline you need to stay on the path even when it's hard. As soon as you have decided this, you will find it a lot easier to stay motivated. Don't forget to reward and congratulate yourself any time you achieve a task that you wanted to achieve without putting it off until later. This can help you associate achieving tasks with a good, positive feeling, setting yourself up for more success in the future.

Since one of the main reasons you want to stop procrastinating is to reach a happier and more joyful existence, don't forget to celebrate when you do something right! And don't forget to enjoy your new levels of productivity and purpose in life.

- **Stick with it till the End:** For those who have a serious procrastination issue, you might find it hard to stay on track during the first month or so of making these changes. Don't worry, that's completely normal. The best way to keep going instead of letting this bother you and stop you is to forgive yourself quickly anytime you make a mistake. If you have started working out each day, for example, and forgot to do it for a few days in a row, realize that you can get right back to it as soon as you've realized you need to.

This is much better than beating yourself up, which will only tempt you to slack off and procrastinate more. This doesn't have to be a big deal or something you dwell on and feel awful about. Feeling guilty will only keep you stuck in your old habits and ways. Sure, it can be a struggle to get the positive momentum going for better habits, but it does get easier and easier the longer you stick with it. Stay with it and prove it to yourself that you are capable and willing to do the work.

Procrastination is all about postponing "for tomorrow" what you need to do today. This happens to everyone, as mentioned earlier in the book, but becomes a real problem when it's an ingrained habit that you take part in on a consistent basis. Perhaps you have been putting off addressing this because you look around and see that it's quite normal and that many people do it. Unfortunately, most people don't realize how detrimental this seemingly harmless little habit can really be. In fact, it can be downright insidious. Essentially, you will feel happier if you stop doing this.

It's up to YOU and only You!

When you start to take action in your life and do what you know you need to do, you can feel good about who you are instead of ashamed. You will no longer have to dwell or worry because you'll know that you've done your best. Only you can make this change; no one can do it for you, and it starts within with a simple choice and commitment. Stop accepting this in your life and commit to doing something about it. You can change. This is the call to action you've been waiting for!

Conclusion

Thank for making it through to the end of *Procrastination: 25 Anti-Procrastination Habits on How to Stop being Lazy and Get Things Done.* Let's hope it was informative and able to provide you with all of the tools you need to become efficient, organized, and disciplined, instead of unhappy and ineffective. A lot of people in the world are victims of their own procrastination habits, so changing yours for the better will put you far ahead of the game by default.

When you stop procrastinating you will begin getting done what you have always dreamed of getting done. You will be free from that lingering guilty feeling that seems to always hang in the back of your mind, and will finally be able to relax. You will be able to achieve the goals that give your life purpose and direction, make commitments and feel good about sticking to them, make others happier, and have better relationships. Doing this will cause your self-confidence to soar and grow constantly. As soon as you decide to give yourself a real chance to change, you will be surprised at how far you can go.

The next step is to follow all 25 tips and stop letting yourself get away with falling off course! Feeling guilty about the time you've wasted is counterproductive and you should instead focus on what you can do *now* to make your life better. You should start timing yourself as you work throughout the day so that you can stay on task, work better, and take breaks as needed.

Following the guidelines in this book will lead you to the life you love and deserve to experience.

Finally, if you found this book useful in any way, a review on Amazon is always appreciated!

www.ingramcontent.com/pod-product-compliance
Lightning Source LLC
Chambersburg PA
CBHW061202180526
45170CB00002B/924